LE CORBUSIER

THE MASTERS OF
WORLD ARCHITECTURE SERIES

UNDER THE GENERAL EDITORSHIP OF WILLIAM ALEX

LE CORBUSIER by Françoise Choay
FRANK LLOYD WRIGHT by Vincent Scully, Jr.
PIER LUIGI NERVI by Ada Louise Huxtable
ANTONIO GAUDI by George R. Collins
LUDWIG MIES VAN DER ROHE by Arthur Drexler
ALVAR AALTO by Frederick Gutheim

le corbusier

by Françoise Choay

George Braziller, Inc.
NEW YORK, 1960

Library of Congress Catalog Card Number: 60-6079

Printed in the United States of America
by R. R. Donnelley & Sons Company

CONTENTS

Text   9

   1. Architecture and Controversy:
     Biographical Notes   9

   2. Rationalism and Mechanism   14

   3. Man, Purpose and Form of Architecture   18

   4. Poetry and Aesthetics   22

The Marseille Block   25

Notes to the Text   27

Plates   33

Selected Bibliography   113

Chronology: Life and Works of Le Corbusier   116

Summary: Main Events in Contemporary Architecture   117

Source of Illustrations   121

Index   123

LE CORBUSIER

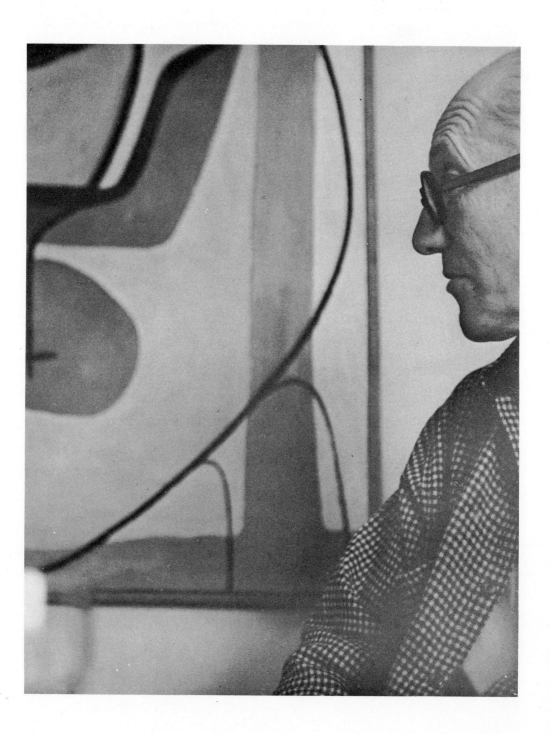

THROUGHOUT his career, ever since he was 30, Le Corbusier has never stopped publishing books and articles—to defend himself, to attack others, at times to put forth general theories, and at times to enlighten us about his intentions or about particular facts. His texts—their style prophetic but sharp and terse, strewn with exclamation points and ellipses, but following a rigorous logic—have exercised an influence in the history of forms comparable only to that of the great theoretical writings of the Renaissance. For those who want to understand Le Corbusier, knowing his written word is as necessary as knowing his architecture.

But his writings are many and abstruse, and under an appearance of simplicity—which has misled a number of critics—hide a great complexity and an essentially dialectic content. Therefore, the aim of this study is to provide a guide which will consider the written and constructed parts of Le Corbusier's output as but two embodiments of the same ideas. What justifies our venture is thus an attempt at synthesis. This is no chronological account, no descriptive analysis, but a search for the meaning, the spirit.

A first chapter will, nevertheless, give the main points of reference on Le Corbusier, the man and his works.

I

ARCHITECTURE AND CONTROVERSY: BIOGRAPHICAL NOTES

The schools are the product of 19th century theories. In a time of complete upheaval they have, with their diplomas, officially applied the brake. They have killed architecture. *

CHARLES EDOUARD JEANNERET was born on October 6, 1887[1] at La-Chaux-de-Fonds[2] in the Swiss Jura Mountains, just 4 kilometers from the French border. In this valley 1,000 meters high, which French refugees have made since the 18th century into the world center of precision watch-making, he received the imprint of a harsh climate and of austere, Protestant principles.

The Jeanneret family, originally from the south of France, had been established in this region since 1350. Charles Edouard's father was a dial-painter—a craft requiring great patience. His mother, *née* Perret, was a musician, and her talent was to be

* Section heading quotations are from the writings of Le Corbusier.

inherited by both her sons, Albert, the musician, and Charles Edouard, the architect, whose style is related to counterpoint. Always sensitive to the poetry of words, Charles Edouard took from one of his ancestors the pseudonym Le Corbusier, with its haughty and slightly emphatic sound.

Following his father's example, Le Corbusier as a child prepared himself for a manual occupation. At 13½ he left elementary school for the La-Chaux-de-Fonds Art School, where he served his apprenticeship as an engraver and chiseler. He was to conserve a love for and first-hand knowledge of the 'materials' with which, throughout his career, he would not be afraid to reestablish contact, as when he himself made the framework for the hollow reliefs of the Marseille Block, or personally sawed the planks for his studio at Cap Martin. But the most important thing he received at the La-Chaux-de-Fonds Professional School was the teaching of an unforgettable man, l'Eplatenier, the only man who really could be considered Le Corbusier's master. L'Eplatenier taught young Le Corbusier the history of art; he conveyed to him his passion for the masterpieces of the past; he turned him towards architecture and gave him the habit he would never lose of drawing and observing from life.[3]

It was on l'Eplatenier's advice that for three years—from 1906 to 1909—Le Corbusier took to the roads of Europe with a knapsack over his shoulder and a sketchbook in his pocket (plate 1). These *Wanderjahre,* rounded out by the long trip on foot which took the young man through "countries reputed to be still intact" from Prague to Serbia, to Roumania, then to Andrinople, Istanbul, Mount Athos, Athens, were more decisive for him than schools and teachers. He became acquainted with the discoveries of folk architecture, both traditional and spontaneous; he discovered the masterpieces of learned architecture and the art of "dimensioning"; finally, he was forever dazzled by Greece, where he got some of the major themes of his work: his way of integrating constructions into the landscape, the human scale and the mastery of light.

When he came to Paris in 1908, Le Corbusier went resolutely to the *atelier* of Auguste Perret, and not the École des Beaux-Arts, with its academic tradition, impervious to the novelty of the age. Later, the school was to take cruel revenge for this disdain.[4] Perret, a public works contractor, was the first great promoter and user of reinforced concrete. He had correctly gauged the importance and the future of the new material, and in 1903 built the first building with a concrete framework, on *rue* Franklin in Paris. At Perret's, Le Corbusier was introduced to this material with which he was later to give the purest lyrical expression. During the fourteen months when, in his own words, he 'worked like a dog' in Perret's studio, the young man received a taste of the quiet courage of a man who, like himself, was self-taught, and had not received diplomas from official schools. It is amusing to note in passing that the two greatest French builders of the 20th century have ignored the Ecole des Beaux-Arts. But Perret belongs to the generation of pioneers (his last historically important work dates from 1919); Le Corbusier will illustrate the first generation of modern architects.

Before the First World War, Le Corbusier spent some months in Germany where he frequented Behrens's studio and became acquainted with the *Werkbund.* But the war interrupted his career, and he spent four years as a teacher at his old school in La-Chaux-de-Fonds. During this period he planned a series of remarkable projects which contain the germ of all his architectural theory. These projects aim at complete pre-fabrication and industrialization of housing: the Domino houses of 1914–1915.

Immediately after the end of the war, Le Corbusier returned to Paris. In 1920, along with Charles Dermée and the painter Amédée Ozenfant, he founded a fighting, avant-garde magazine 'L'Esprit Nouveau.'[5] This was not only an architectural magazine: all the arts had their place, and also the sciences, sociology, psychology and biology. Among the collaborators were to be found the names of Maurice Raynal, the critic; Albert Jeanneret and Darius Milhaud, the musicians; R. Allendy, the psychoanalyst; Jean Lurçat, the painter, and H. Hertz, the sociologist-historian. As for Le Corbusier, he published a series of articles dedicated mainly to town-planning and to the birth of what was not yet called industrial design. Some of these articles were later (in 1923) to be published in a volume which is probably the controversial architect's major book, *Towards a New Architecture.* For his magazine, Le Corbusier fought, organized, solic-ited funds, fulminated. He struggled through difficulties, but this activity was the result in his case of a deep-seated need for action, for participation in collective life. His is the soul of a prophet; *Crusade* is the significant title of one of his books; building is not enough for him. Besides, the originality and the uncompromising nature of his ideas were always to keep him from doing much building, especially during the early part of his career. Some of his most important works will never be realized, and will remain in the project or town-planning stage; but the young architects of today know them by heart, and they have played a theoretical role of first importance.

Two years after founding 'L'Esprit Nouveau,' Le Corbusier opened the studio at 35 *rue de Sèvres* with his cousin Pierre Jeanneret, a quiet man who always stayed in the background but who played a very important role in the conception and the realiza-tion of Le Corbusier's work, and their two names should not be dissociated at least until 1945. Generations of architects[6] have been—and are still—nurtured in the *rue de Sèvres* studio, and from the beginning one could hear many languages spoken, be-cause Le Corbusier's reputation outside France grew rapidly. In France, where he took out citizenship in 1930, his name is even today synonymous with scandal. In his *rue de Sèvres* studio, he does not teach in a doctrinaire manner; neither is the studio compa-rable to a *Bauhaus* dominated by the serene and essentially didactic figure of Gropius. The master is not patient; he is rough, at times despotic. But in his eyes youth is the most precious of qualities, and when nights of passionate work and discussion go into a project, all become equals; it is the most complete form of collaboration.

As to the works which have come out of the *rue de Sèvres* studio for thirty-seven years, one can consider them as belonging to two periods: before and after the Second World War. This division is more a matter of method than of any real existence of two different stages in an evolution which was constant, but slow and continuous.

Immediately after the First World War, Le Corbusier had hopes of participating in the industrial reconstruction of the country and in its town-planning on a large scale according to the new principles. His hopes were disappointed. His activity in France was mainly in housing; not the housing of the many, as he would have liked, but the construction of villas and private mansions, akin in style and spirit to the contemporary works of the French architects Mallet-Stevens and Pierre Charreau, or the Dutch architect Rietveld. The most interesting of these houses are the Vaucresson villa (1922) (plate 2), the Ozenfant house in Paris (1922), the La Roche house in Paris (1923) (plate 3), the Cook house in Paris (1926), the Garches villa (1927) (plate 5), the Savoye house at Poissy (1929–1931) (plates 6–8). Of them, only the La Roche house, on Doctor Blanche Square, remains today as it was conceived. In 1925, the help of a rich industrialist who shared his views on working-class housing enabled him to build the Pessac Workers' City, near Bordeaux (plate 10). But this type of housing, which did not try to affect false local color, was ardently opposed by the municipal and provincial authorities: as a result of their criticism, the Pessac development could not be supplied with water and for six years it was forbidden for anyone to live there.

During this same period, in spite of it all, Le Corbusier was putting up a number of great buildings: the Centrosoyus in Moscow (1929–1935) (plate 11) which, still in perfect condition, today houses the Ministry of Light Industries; the Refuge City of the Salvation Army in Paris (1920–1933), with its first radical use of the glass wall (considerably modified since), and, finally, his greatest success, the Swiss Pavilion at the Paris *Cité Universitaire* (plates 12–15). This last building was considered scandalous at the time it was built, and remained the only daring building on the grounds until the recent construction of the Brazilian Pavilion (plate 16). In 1938, Le Corbusier took part in drawing up plans for a building finished in 1943, and which is one of the manifestos of modern architecture: the Ministry of National Education in Rio de Janeiro (plate 17).

But his uncompleted projects are even more numerous. One must cite, on the one hand, the plans for large buildings: the League of Nations Palace in Geneva (1927), received first prize but was later rejected as a result of intrigue on the pretext that the plans had not been drawn in China ink, and later adapted by the contest winners; the Palace of the Soviets (1931) (plate 9), rejected because the rulers of the U.S.S.R. were embarking on the road which would lead them to abandon progressive architecture[7] and return to a traditionalist and pompous style. On the other hand, Le Corbusier made known his projects for town-planning, which were later to become celebrated: the Voisin Plan for Paris (1922–1930–1936) (plate 18), the Plan for Barcelona (1932), the projects for Algiers (1931–1934–1938) (plates 20–22, 24), Stockholm and Anvers (1933), etc. The theoretical thinking behind these plans led Le Corbusier, in 1928, to sponsor the International Congresses of Modern Architecture, the C.I.A.M., which were to play a most important role in the history of modern architecture and urbanism. The first congress took place at the Sarraz castle in Switzerland in 1928. The fourth was held in Athens, and led to the formulation and adoption of principles which reveal Le Corbusier's influence, and which he was later to edit and develop anonymously during the German occupation. They were published in 1942 under the name of Athens Charter, a breviary of contemporary town-planning.

The period after the Second World War rekindled Le Corbusier's hopes of 1919. They were to be disappointed in the same way. He had practically no part in the reconstruction of the country. His two magnificent plans for Rochelle-Pallice and St. Dié, which grouped dwellings in vertical cities of 1,500 to 2,000 inhabitants, integrated them in green zones and redistributed the centers of activity in a rational way, were ignored or rejected. The St. Dié plan (plate 23) in 1946 was exhibited throughout the United States, where it was considered the symbol of French rebirth. But the town of St. Dié has become one of the most platitudinous of French achievements, thus fulfilling the wishes of the local press that 'brick might triumph over the skyscraper.'

Nevertheless, the intelligence and the tenacity of two ministers of the Reconstruction, Raoul Dautry, then Claudius Petit, was to allow Le Corbusier to realize at 60 (1946–1952) his dream of a vertical city, nurtured since 1922. It was the Radiant City of Marseille, built against winds and tides in an atmosphere of incomprehension, symbolized by its local nickname: 'the nincompoop's house.' The Marseille prototype, a very expensive experiment, was to be followed by another version, this time a project subsidized by the state, the Radiant City of Nantes-Rezé. Then followed the Berlin unit, built for the 1957 Interbau and truncated by the local entrepreneurs, and after that, the units currently under construction at Meaux and at Briey-la-Forêt.

At the same time he was busy with these vertical cities, Le Corbusier built some of his best-executed private mansions, notably the Jaoul houses at Neuilly (plates 25–27), the Sarabhai (plates 28, 29) or Shodan villas at Ahmedabad in India. He also devoted his talent to other great human activities, building the Duval works at St. Dié (1946–1951) (plates 30, 31), the Tokyo museum (plate 32), inaugurated in 1959, the Philips pavilion[8] (plates 34, 35) at the Brussels Fair (1958), and the convent of La Tourette (plates 75–78, 84) near Lyon (finished in 1959), the austerity and rigor of which contrast with the less controlled lyricism of the Ronchamp chapel (plates 36–43) (finished in 1955), a sculptural watchtower built in the foothills of the Vosges.

Finally, the work accomplished by Le Corbusier in Chandigarh, India, occupies a special place. In 1950, the Indian government got in touch with him about the building of a new political capital for the Punjab, and in 1951 Le Corbusier was officially entrusted with directing the planning and construction of the town of Chandigarh, created on an empty plain at the foot of the Himalayas. He was helped in this task by the English architects Jane Drew and Maxwell Fry, and by Pierre Jeanneret, with whom (since 1940) he is no longer associated.

While his three collaborators occupied themselves primarily with the dwellings for the 500,000 inhabitants of the future town, Le Corbusier applied his town-planning theories and personally attacked the problem of the administrative center, the Capitol (plates 44, 46, 47). This contains essentially the High Court of Justice (completed) (plate 45), the Palace of the Seven Ministries (completed) (plate 54), the Government Palace and the Parliament. These rough concrete buildings, unusual and sculptural, mark the peak of Le Corbusier's work so far. Completely free of formulas, as well as of any popular influence, they are adapted to the climatic imperatives through the use of giant sun-breaks (plate 56) and umbrella-roofs in the shape of concrete shells (plate

51). They are also related—by certain features such as gentle, sloping indoor ramps (plates 52, 53) and the interplay of levels (plate 57)—to the architect's earliest works; and they bear witness both to Le Corbusier's faithfulness to himself and to the permanent spirit of invention which have made him at once an architect and an incomparable artist.

II

RATIONALISM AND MECHANISM

I had given the house its fundamental importance, calling it 'a machine to live in,' thus exacting from it the complete and perfect answer to a well-set question.

HIS RATIONALISM is the aspect through which Le Corbusier has most often been introduced to the public. For a large number of his critics,[9] sympathetic or otherwise, he remains the theoretician who perfected a rigorous system and whose works are subjected to a cold, standardizing logic and an uncompromising functionalism.

This partial vision is partially true. By temperament Le Corbusier is a Cartesian: logical reasoning is the framework, the foundation, if not the objective of all his enterprises. But in Le Corbusier's hands rationalism is also a weapon, a favored instrument of combat, which makes him define and diagram his thinking in trenchant formulas to justify each of his plastic gestures. This attitude often assumes an aggressive and caricature-like aspect, and one cannot assess it correctly except within its polemic context.

The mechanical revolution has upset our means of production, of knowledge and communication. During his childhood and youth, Le Corbusier witnessed the invention of the automobile, the cinema, the telegraph, the telephone and the airplane. Later, the First World War caused technology to take another leap forward. Yet this veritable mutation of means, and consequently of needs, was not followed by any change in the structure of our everyday setting, the city or dwelling place. Their lack of adaptation to their new function constitutes a scandalous situation for the thinking man: 20th century man lives in false surroundings built on outdated truths. Le Corbusier will fight for the architectural revolution.

In order to do this, he starts by a destructive operation, an unmercifully rational analysis of all the blemishes in our contemporary setting. From 1920 through 1959 (since the situation has evolved but has not changed radically), without ever allowing himself to be moved by local color or aestheticism,[10] he has denounced them from both the structural and the technological aspects. His attacks are concentrated particularly on the modern phenomenon of the proliferation of towns. First, the structure of these 'stone deserts' makes them perishable because of their inadaptability. *Circulation,* adapted to the means of transportation of another age (carriages, horses), is becoming more and more difficult: bottlenecks, waste of time, mingling of different speeds, interference of pedestrians with mechanical transportation. *The placing of functions* (commerce, industry, administration, dwellings) is haphazard and wasteful. *The placing of buildings* along 'corridor streets' is unhealthy (traffic noises, no sun, no vegetation); *their dimensions* are insufficient; even in New York the skyscrapers are timid, and the city is 'a spectacular catastrophe'[11]; *the dispersion of garden-towns* is doomed from an economic standpoint; the dwelling itself, *the living cell,* too large but uncomfortable, is chock-full of useless, finicky objects, a jumble inherited from a past age. On top of this, the building technique employed in towns has remained at an archaic and handicraft stage; it contrasts with that used for dams, airplane hangars—in a word, with all the constructions that one considers devoid of nobility, and which are the only ones in harmony with our times. Le Corbusier's preliminary destruction does not stop at the level of critical analysis: he formally proposes that existing cities be pruned, and that their centers that are unfit for traffic be demolished. Only monuments of historical interest deserve to be preserved: the plans for Paris (from 1922 to 1956) erase the "picturesque" but unsanitary quarters; the Project for Algiers cuts deep into the lower Casbah; the proposals for New York do away with some of the present skyscrapers.

After destruction, construction. Once the old pattern is destroyed, the new can be entirely re-thought. The method consists of *defining, classifying* and *putting in order* needs and functions, and the logician does not hesitate to begin with the most general of functions. The whole of human activities can be summed up in: *living, working, circulating, cultivating one's body and mind.*[12] These functions, in their turn, can be arranged according to the three types of human establishments which are both necessary and sufficient: *the radio-concentric city,* a place of exchanges which groups the functions of leadership, administration, commerce, handicraft and thinking; *the linear industrial city,* a place of transformations established along the routes for the passage of goods, and finally, the *unit of agricultural exploitation.* Each of these forms possesses its typical structure, which serves as a logical framework universally valid in establishing concrete plans. The radio-concentric city is built vertically, so as to concentrate and bring together as much as possible the different sectors of individualized activity: business city, civic center, dwelling zones. Examples of this type are the project for Algiers; the project for St. Dié, with its civic center, its five units of vertical dwellings and, on the other side of the river, the industrial town; the project for Paris (plate 19) where business is grouped in four gigantic buildings situated in the green zone of the city on the right bank of the Seine between Montmartre and les Buttes-Chaumont, while the governmental city is placed on the left. The linear city is divided into parallel belts which include, on one side of a turnpike reserved for motor vehicles, factories placed in green areas and roads (earth, rail, water) for the passage of goods and, on the other side, isolated by a green curtain, the dwelling sector. It is according to this pattern that the plans for La Rochelle-Pallice were drawn up. Finally, the units for rural exploitation are 're-vitalized' by means of cooperative centers consisting of silos, a store, a repair shop, a club, schools, a town hall and collective building.[13]

The three establishments are served by a traffic system which classifies motor vehicle traffic according to speed, and separates the pedestrian: in its more elaborate form, it is known as the *7 V's system* (V = road) applied in Chandigarh. The hierarchy of roads starts with the vast V1, an artery with an inter-national or inter-urban role, and ends with the fine capillary system of V7 in the green zone reserved for children, for schools and sports, the V5 and V6 being essentially interior roads for reduced speed serving the housing units. Thus, different sectors of different towns are completely reorganized in terms of two standards: function and traffic. In turn, they will be further differentiated according to the rational typologies of the factory, the dwelling and the green zone. So great is Le Corbusier's need for logical organization that, having to lay out the vast Capitol of Chandigarh, he divides the vegetation to be used into six categories, each of which receives a precise function.

Among the possible forms of the dwelling, the vertical one is the favorite: it is the housing unit, the vertical commune of from 1,500 to 2,000 inhabitants, recommended in 1922 in 'The Plan for a Contemporary City of Three Million Inhabitants,' but realized for the first time only in 1952 in Marseille[14] (plates 58–61). The vertical unit follows a rigorous logic: it saves scarce and costly urban land; it gives everybody a favorable orientation; it enables all inhabitants to benefit from the help of the grouped common services. In its turn, the *cell* in the interior of the unit is divided up into individual and collective functions. These are separated and arranged in a hierarchy: the spaces allotted to life in common are vaster and more noble, and often double the height of the others. The spaces where one doesn't spend much time are reduced to a minimum, like those moving cells (plates 63, 64), a cabin on a ship and a sleeping compartment on a train (plate 65). In this Le Corbusier enjoys the precise adaptation of the organ to its function. Finally, furniture[15] is eliminated in favor of *equipment* corresponding to the functions of the cell: cooking, hygiene, sleep, tidying, sitting.

This structural system, which develops logically from the level of the land to that of the individual dwelling cell, must be achieved by new techniques in building and industrial production. As far as construction is concerned, Le Corbusier has brought out the logic of steel and reinforced concrete. These materials have produced a revolution in the art of building: the *independent skeleton* of building. From now on, the house rests on supporting piles; it does not need supporting walls. For Le Corbusier, the theoretician, the logical consequences of the independent skeleton are called: *free plan, pillar foundation* (pilotis), *glass wall* with integral *sunbreaks* (brise-soleil), *roof terrace.* Some of these elements (roof terrace, pillars) already existed in more or less advanced forms; others have been handled brilliantly by a number of contemporary architects: Gropius, since 1913, and later Mies van der Rohe, have been incomparable masters of the glass wall; Aalto is celebrated for the freedom and imagination of his plans. Yet it seems that Le Corbusier is the inventor of these essential organs of modern architecture: this is not untrue if one thinks that he was the first to name them,[16] to realize that they were necessary, and to develop their theory.

But he didn't stop at theories. Since 1923 (the La Roche House), he has shown a real virtuosity in *the freedom of his plans,* never enslaved to conventions or to exterior symmetry, but tied to an internal logic. The plan is the expression of the master idea. In the case of individual houses, he expresses at the same time a special purpose, as, for example, to exhibit a collection of modern art in the case of the La Roche house, or to provide a place for relaxation in the open air in the case of the Savoye house at Poissy (plate 8), and a revolution in the way of living: a single living-room, of double height, communicating with a particularly large kitchen which becomes the 'cockpit of the house'; no separation of bedroom and bathroom; utilization of stairs, hearths, closet space as elements of classification of diverse functions, as seen especially in the Jaoul house (plates 25–27). The freedom of the plan is also manifest in the large buildings. We cite only the ingeniousness of the museum of continuous growth, conceived in 1931 on the plan of a square spiral[17] (plate 33).

In his re-structuration of the dwelling plan, Le Corbusier is brought to suppress, at least partially, the closed ground floor. The underground piles become visible, become 'pilotis'[18] and project the house into the sky, to free the ground for pedestrians (and not for automobiles), to allow vegetation and the sun under the house. The pillar (pilotis) which appears for the first time in 1922 in the plans for the Citrohan house, will become one of the constants of Le Corbusier's architecture, but its form will evolve from the thin cylindric columns of Poissy (plate 8) to the powerful shanks of Marseille (plates 61, 70, 71) or the Brazil Pavilion (1959) (plate 16).

The old supporting wall can be replaced by a weightless screen-wall. The traditional window will disappear. In order to proclaim its death sentence, Le Corbusier lights his first houses by cutting long *continuous bands* in the light masonry of the walls: these bands that one finds in the Cook house (plate 4), the villa at Garches (plate 5) or the Savoye house (plate 8), have the value of a manifesto, but they are soon to become entirely glassed walls: these are the south facade of the Swiss Pavilion at the Paris *Cité Universitaire* (plate 13), and then the first completely closed glass wall with an exterior surface of over 11,000 square feet, at the Salvation Army's Refuge City (1933). Indeed, from this time on Le Corbusier conceives of glass work as a strictly visual "organ": the functions of ventilation and temperature regulation must be assured by air conditioning, the procurer of 'exact air.' Unfortunately, air conditioning is usually too expensive to be accepted by clients, even when the client happens to be the Soviet government, as in the case of the Centrosoyus; besides, the sun has proved a redoubtable enemy in summer. In 1933, Le Corbusier invents the logical complement of the glass wall, the *sunbreak,* the dimensions of which are calculated with reference to the sun's course on the horizon, and which is designed to control its effects. It will be put into practice for the first time six years later, when the architect collaborates in the Ministry of Education building in Rio de Janeiro (plate 17), built by Costa, Leao, Moreira, Niemeyer and Reidy. Later, the sunbreak will take different forms at St. Dié, at Marseille, where it undergoes metamorphosis into a loggia (plates 66, 67), and, finally, at Chandigarh, where, calculated with the help of a subtle climate graph, it reaches a depth of 1.40 meters in the facade of the Court of Justice (plate 50). The sunbreak thus becomes one of the means of renovating tropical architecture in South America and in India.

Finally, the logic of concrete allows Le Corbusier the systematic construction of terraced roofs, which conquers new spaces for the house. In conformity with old rural practices, waterproofing is improved by a bed of sod which introduces a new element, the suspended *garden,* which may be found in Poissy and also, twenty years later, in St. Dié and Ahmedabad.

All these key organs of modern architecture are, with Le Corbusier, the fruit of radical rationalization. The same logical radicalism led him, during his first years of activity, to use new, intellectually very attractive materials and procedures, but which did not stand the test of time. The result, in some cases, has been a deterioration and a dilapidation which makes one forget the formal perfection of the buildings.[19] These misfortunes will later lead Le Corbusier to the aesthetic of raw materials which contain no possible surprise, a solution towards which he is also impelled by his temperament.

In general, one could say that Le Corbusier is no technician. But in order to finish with his construction procedures, one ought to say that he has since 1914 predicted the application of industrial production methods to building, and proposed the construction of series of houses of prefabricated and standardized elements, for instance the Domino houses (1914–1915) and the Citrohan houses[20] of 1920 and 1922. It was in connection with these houses that Le Corbusier used the expression 'machine to live in,' which has given rise to repeated misunderstandings, and has taxed him with the label of functionalism.[21] What Le Corbusier meant by this was that the house could be produced by industry with the same perfection as could the machines to move about in, for example. It was not a question of reducing to a simple mechanism functions whose rich cultural meaning Le Corbusier had always underlined.

This expression also translated the need for the formal purity found in the design of machines, in the image of which he conceives all the useful objects to be found in day-to-day life. It was not by accident that Le Corbusier in 1918 adopted the cubist movement, and that he was a friend of the painter Fernand Léger. During the 20's, his cubist, or purist, aesthetic[22] coincides in an ambiguous way with his logic, the shape of his houses with that of the pictures he has painted in his studio since 1919 (plates 79–82). Cubism, 'one of the decisive moments of the general revolution,' seeks a truth of the object the way architecture seeks a truth of the function. There is, of course, a sort of functionalism here, but Le Corbusier's architecture does not limit itself to it. That is what the next chapters will try to prove.

III

MAN, PURPOSE AND FORM OF ARCHITECTURE

The 20th century hasn't built for men; it has built for money.

ONE CAN imagine some architects, yesterday Gaudí, today the great artist Mies van der Rohe, moved by a sort of aesthetic instinct, and building for the pure joy of building. For Le Corbusier, on the other hand, who never dissociated town planning from architecture, building is essentially a social action aimed at man and at the solution of his problems. Le Corbusier's work bears the mark of both rationalism and the image of man. But this image plays a complex role.

18

From an ethical standpoint, Le Corbusier is the spiritual son of the enlightened philosophers of the 18th century, and of the socialist utopians who were their 19th century heirs. The humanitarian logic of his work develops around the following postulates: men are all *equal,* endowed with the same fundamental needs, no matter what their cultural levels; because of this, they all have a right to *happiness;* this must be assured by the *progress* of technique, put at the service of the architect. His large hedonistic vocabulary,[23] the role he gives to collective and family life, and the future he predicts for man in a mechanical civilization, evoke the name of Fourier, whose theories have effectively played a role in Le Corbusier's ideological formation.[24]

It is thus from this point of view that he undertakes to define the basic needs of universal man. We shall place them on three levels. At the first level, which is almost purely physical, each man must, in his dwelling, where progress will make him spend more and more time, enjoy the key materials of town-planning: sun, space, vegetation.[25] These satisfy man's natural animal needs denied by modern life. Although fascinated by the machine, Le Corbusier has always remained the son of the harsh valleys of the Jura. He is one of those who contributed towards establishing the modern cult of the sun: more than elements required by the logic of construction, the glass wall and the solarium-terraces are means of distributing the sun.

At the second level, defined by the exigencies of psychosomatic comfort, the needs of universal man are: thermic regulation (by air conditioning); ventilation; sonic insulation. The problem of ventilation has preoccupied Le Corbusier since the 30's when, in the Barcelona development (1933) or the House on the Ocean at Mathes, he created systems of air draughts with the help of small adjustable openings in the facades. These studies led to the creation of a new element in modern architecture, the *ventilator,* which will take its finished form after the research done for Chandigarh.[26] At the Brazilian Pavilion (plate 83), at the Jaoul house, at La Tourette (plate 84), as well as at the Chandigarh Secretariat (plates 54, 55), the ventilators take the form of long, narrow boxes closed by shutters and placed in the glass wall of the windows, the function of which, let us remind you, is purely visual. One of Le Corbusier's main concerns is soundproofing, and the means of providing individual isolation in the midst of the collectivity of his huge vertical cities. Compared to most of the recent European housing condemned to noise by architects more interested in facades than in essential comfort, the quality of their soundproofing[27] is perhaps one of the most remarkable features of Le Corbusier's apartment buildings. At Marseille, for instance, where the units are inserted in the concrete skeleton like bottles in a rack, sonic isolation has been obtained by insulating each cell of the skeleton with lead boxes.

At the third level, an entirely cultural one, Le Corbusier proposes the types of ideal dwellings for universal man: the vertical city, with interior streets (plate 68) on which apartments open, and with the common services which range from the automatic laundry and the shops placed in a specialized street, to the kindergartens, to the gymnasium and the theater; and the individual unit or apartment, characterized by its smallness and the functional classification of its space, which differentiates collective life from individual life.[28] This third level constitutes the sore point of Le Corbusier's system, where it seems difficult to defend the architect against his detractors. Human individualism and particularism seem to be on the cultural level, as well as on an individual level, a basic datum not susceptible to integration in a universal structure. The Marseille dwelling unit has numbered among its occupants detractors and partisans, equally fierce and convinced: they were not all similarly disposed, prepared and formed to live there. A *Provençal,* a friend of full-fledged kitchens and ground-level houses, could not make himself live in the skies and utilize the minuscule kitchen-cockpit (plate 63), while an architect or a professor was perfectly happy.

In order to live in rigorously classified spaces like those of the dwelling unit or the luxury individual dwellings, built according to the same spatial norms by Le Corbusier, one must have an urbane outlook,[29] and a certain intellectual level or a special mental disposition. How many people are capable of living and living well, as Le Corbusier does every summer at Cap Martin, in a cabin (cabanon) of 170 square feet?[30] To conclude, it seems that in his suggestions for a universal dwelling, Le Corbusier, versed in abstractions, denies the empirical diversity of man and projects personal abilities onto a universal scale.[31]

Yet the image of man plays a singularly concrete role when, in an anthropocentric perspective inherited from ancient Greece, it enters into Le Corbusier's plastic as an absolute unit of measurement of all things built. 'One must always try to find the *human scale,*'[32] says Le Corbusier. One must never trust the drawing and the arbitrary measurements of plans, because 'an architecture must be walked through, traversed';[33] it is made to be seen by our human eye placed at 63 inches from the ground.[34] This constant preoccupation with *what appears* in concrete experience is the reason why Le Corbusier's architecture is never scant nor 'unmeasured' and, independently of its dimension, is always at the scale of man. Therefore, on the one hand the architect deforms and plays on the illusions of eyesight, at times in order to make modest spaces loom larger,[35] as in the case of the Swiss Pavilion (plate 14), or at Ronchamp, especially through the ascending curve of the roof (plate 37), which rises from 15 to 33 feet, or else, in the cabin, thanks to the play of mirrors and paintings on the walls; at times in order to make vast spaces look smaller, as at Chandigarh, where he uses tiers of water mirrors to bring together buildings which seem too far apart (plates 45, 48). The measurements and the gestures of the human body serve as a unit of measurement: an hour of walking is the unit of town-planning, while the height of a man, his pace, the reach of his arm, his foot, his thumb, and so on, will serve to calculate the size of doors, window, sunbreaks or pillars.

That is how Le Corbusier was led to conceive a double scale of proportions, derived from human dimensions, and which was to attain its completed form in 1948 under the name of Modulor[36] (plates 85–87). From now on, this will serve to calculate the elements of all Le Corbusier's buildings, from the Marseille Block to the Chandigarh Capitol, through Ronchamp or the Brazilian Pavilion.[37] In this way will be measured the noblest elements, like the musical glass panes of La Tourette or of the Chandigarh ministries, and the most humble elements—ventilator, doorknob, bannister or pavement.[38] Thus, not only will modern man, who feels himself a stranger in the monuments or dwellings of 19th and 20th century architecture, find in the buildings of Le Corbusier a wonderful feeling of security, of familiarity, a sort of happiness involving all his movements, but the buildings themselves will appear as harmonious wholes, the different modules of which are tied to one another like the score of a symphony. Such, for example, is the facade of the St. Dié factory (plate 30), built on three different rhythms (the spreading out of the skeleton, grill-work of sunbreaks, lattice-work of the glass wall), similarly provided by the Modulor.

Finally, this chapter would be incomplete if we did not present the human image (so far envisaged essentially in its physical and natural aspect) under a philosophical light, which allows it to be opposed to other creatures and creations of nature. The dignity of man lies precisely in his cultural and 'de-natured' being, and this conception leads Le Corbusier to a relationship with nature entirely different from those entertained by, for example, the architects of the American Californian school. For the latter, the aim is to have nature penetrate the house so completely as not to be able to tell where each begins and ends. For Le Corbusier, on the contrary, there is no inter-penetration. The house is an assertion of man *in the face of* nature; if landscape is an essential element of architecture, it penetrates under the pillars or through the windows, like a *spectacle*, while the building itself gives to its location and to natural architecture a superior value and order.[39] One will notice especially the vertical and horizontal elements which on the terraces and the roofs of Le Corbusier's houses serve to structure and frame the landscape.

This same domineering conception of man leads Le Corbusier to use the most brutally natural materials. Contrary to a general opinion, the poet of concrete passionately loves wood, slate and stone. He built the Errazuris house in Chile completely in stone and wood, like the Mathes house in France. He uses stone any time he can, in the villa of Madame de Mandrot, in the Swiss Pavilion, in the Brazilian Pavilion, in St. Dié. These raw natural elements, loved and conceived as such, serve to make the human miracle of the mathematics which orders them appear even more striking. They have no value in themselves, but only by relation to the calculating mind which they glorify while opposing it, and which in its turn confers upon them a savor forgotten by civilized man.

But beyond his part in this spiritual imposition of order, man is valued down to his most humble gesture. Any trace of the human individual and of his hand acquires for Le Corbusier a moving value. Thus he highly prizes beautiful stone masonry, and also nearly always uses in his most beautiful buildings an artisan capable of doing the finest carpentry or masonry work.[40] Thus also he gives value to the accidents or malforma-tions inherent in concrete and which tell its story.[41] In doing this, Le Corbusier approaches, strangely enough, a tendency of contemporary avant-garde aesthetics,[42] and leaves the classical shores of post-Cubism, which he clings to, however, in his painting.

IV

But where does sculpture start, or painting, or architecture? The body of the building is the expression of the three major arts in one.

WHEN ONE has added up the rationalist and human factors, one hasn't yet got Le Corbusier's formula. The main factor is missing, of which the other two are only the support and the justification: the poetic factor.

This disinterested search for beauty which began forty years ago has led the architect to consecrate a part of his activity every day to the painting of pictures, some of which are in the collection of international museums. Later he developed a passion for tapestry, and recently for sculpture.[43] But these activities cannot be separated from architecture. A precursor of what is today called 'the integration of arts in architecture,' Le Corbusier has always liked to finish his buildings with frescoes, as in the Swiss Pavilion, reliefs, as at Marseille, or paintings, or tapestries, as in Chandigarh, where they muffle the noises of the Seven Courts of Justice, or by conceiving the composition of certain elements like the Ronchamp doors.[44] Yet Le Corbusier's architecture itself must be considered a plastic, poetic activity.

For him architecture is, first of all, the organization of masses; he has given it a celebrated and meaningful definition: 'Architecture is the masterly, correct and magnificent play of the forms of light.' But, with time, these forms and their way of being assembled have evolved towards an ever-greater freedom and lyricism, the equivalent of which one finds in the development of the architect's painting.[45] The resistance of beautiful cubes intelligently perforated is offered to the light of day in the houses at Garches and Vaucresson and the Cook house. The aesthetic coincides with logic, and by this very fact the interiors are diversified, and look more sculptured than the exteriors. Around 1930, when the painter was enriching his vocabulary, until then limited to simple objects—bottles, decanters and glasses—the clay model of the Centrosoyus resembles a sculpture by Lipschitz, and the back of the Swiss Pavilion is folded in a generous curve. But it is after World War II that the architectural plastic of Le Corbusier acquires all its generosity: the forms remain simple, but they combine in marvellous inventions. Thus are born the admirable sculptures which are called Ronchamp, with the double curve of its roof (plate 37), shaped like a concrete shell, and its inclined walls; the High Court of Chandigarh (plates 48–50), the facade of which, furrowed by the concrete sun-breaks, is a light trap, while the ascendant heavenward movement of the parasol-shaped roof is balanced by the serene verticality of the pillars at the entrance portal; in the Brazilian Pavilion of the Paris Cité Universitaire, the buildings literally fit into each other, with the little annex building passing underneath the pillars (pilotis) of the dormitories and thus dividing naturally into two curved branches (plate 16). As Le Corbusier grows older, each architectural element becomes an opportunity for sculpture,[46] although it never loses its function. Thus the ventilation chimneys (plate 73), the roof (plate 74), the fire stair at the north facade (plate 60) and the powerful pillars of the Marseille Block (plate 71) are as many expressive sculptures.

In his play with forms, the architect uses light[47] as a real substance which helps to animate the buildings with permanent life. If outside it breaks violently against the pillars or the sunbreaks, inside it is manipulated with infinite subtlety, unobtrusively introduced into the vital parts of the building so as, for example, to shadow a stairway against the wall, in order to make the builder's intentions obvious. In his last works one will note especially the openings which penetrate the massive walls of the High Court, or those which limit the flight of stairs in the Secretariat, and the openings made in the walls of the Sarabhai villa in Ahmedabad (plates 28, 29). But the masterpiece in interior lighting is probably attained at Ronchamp, by the combination of all lateral openings[48] (plate 41) and the open space of a few inches which separates the roof from the walls (plate 42).

Finally, like the Greeks of ancient times, the sculptor has not been afraid of color-washing his works in vivid colors. These have different functions: at times to complete the free plan and to accentuate its intentions, by causing a wall to disappear, or by emphasizing another one, as in the La Roche house or the Jaoul house, at other times, to accentuate the imperfections of the building and draw attention to certain defects, as at Marseille; at times to give an intrinsic element of violence and of warmth to facades, as in Chandigarh (Court of Justice) or at the Shodan villa, or to create a hearth of spiritual intensity in the interiors (Ronchamp, for example)[49] (plate 43).

These analyses of the purely poetic aspect of Le Corbusier's plastic art show the determinant role of concrete in the great architect's work: he has been able to mould it in shapes which bronze itself would not have permitted the sculptor, to perforate it to his liking, and to paint it. Yet, the way he has utilized this essentially modern material belongs to an aesthetic which was that of archaic arts and high cultures for which our epoch is nostalgic, and whose brutal authenticity it regrets.[50] Le Corbusier's solutions to construction always look massive, virile and elemental. His simple volumes, cubes, cylinders and pyramids contrast with those chosen by other great artists of concrete, Nervi or, even more, Laffaille and Candela, who use this material in tension, with the rigorous economy which shows a complex dynamic. The Marseille pillars and, still more so, those of the Brazilian house, are more powerful than is necessary.[51] But they have a function of expression like that of the exterior fire stair in Marseille. Its massiveness can be contrasted to the lightness of the one conceived by Nervi for the UNESCO Secretariat in Paris. The difference between these two types of architecture is the same as that discovered by Le Corbusier between the Roman constructions with their primary forms and the Gothic constructions with their complex geometry.[52]

This plastic handling of masses and elemental forms hides no surprises. Its *frankness* is total, like its refusal of any dissimulation. As years pass, the skeleton shows more and more. From the outside, the buildings are readily readable, as for example the facade of the High Court of Chandigarh, where one can instantly perceive the location of the different courts of different ranks, or the exterior projection of the Brazilian Pavilion's staircase. Inside, the seams are not hidden: thus the ductwork of the heating system in the Swiss Pavilion passes through the hall where a plastic role is demanded of it, while enormous concrete beams can be seen in the ceiling of St. Dié (plate 31). There is a rigorous correspondence between exterior and interior, priority being given significantly to the interior. As to the material, it is no more dissimulated than the structures: Le Corbusier exposes without shame the concrete, the stone masonry or the simple brick in the interior of his buildings.[53]

Thus, this taste for truth is often identical with that of *brutality*. The architect loves rough materials, un-polished, not de-natured. If by chance, as in Ronchamp, or for the pillars of the High Court, he coats masonry, he sprays it on with a cement gun which gives the walls a rough and granular skin. Le Corbusier has been the aesthetical promoter of raw unfinished concrete: at times the formwork has been beautiful and carefully done, at times mediocre. This is of little importance, for their imperfection and that of their form work is the moving and authentic trace of human limitation, but also of the kingdom of the living. Finally, materials, like colors, have no intrinsic value. They are exalted by means of form, color and *contrast*. Le Corbusier loves the violent oppositions of stone and concrete, of stone and wood, of stone and glass. In this last case, he likes confronting them without intermediaries, and obtains striking effects when in the undulated glass walls of the Ministries at Chandigarh, at La Tourette or at the Brazilian Pavilion, for example, he inserts glass *directly* into the rough concrete of the pillars,[54] without the intermediary of any casing, but simply with the help of mastic.

Yet these materials, these forms, and these brutal, almost primitive contrasts are distributed with extreme refinement: complex modulation and the correct dimensioning of all parts of the buildings, mastery of light, concern for the most infinitesimal detail,[55] the invention and the scrupulously careful use of new, logical elements, introduce the subtle mediations of the mind into the heart of brutality. Of this permanent counterpoint between the rough and the elaborate, sustained by a further counterpoint between modern techniques and materials and ancient techniques and materials, is born in Le Corbusier's architecture a tension which leads us to delight.

This dialectic, or rather, symphonic character of a work which has been able to reconcile discordant themes into a superior harmony, embraces all the teaching of Le Corbusier, whose logical creations many architects of today have transformed into academic affectation, and whose brutality they have erected in dogma. Having passionately understood and loved the age of the machine into which he was born, and having built 'for the greatest number,' he has proved that it is possible to reconcile with universal standardization the purest poetry, whose source he finds in certain original values that avant-garde plastic art is beginning to rediscover today. Le Corbusier's greatest contribution to 20th century architecture is probably that of having rediscovered man, who had become lost in the frenetic development of technique.

THE MARSEILLE BLOCK

IF THE Chandigarh buildings represent the climax of Le Corbusier's plastic work, the Marseille Block is the summation and symbol of all the theories concerning town planning and dwellings, and also one of the most important social and architectural events of the 20th century. This makes it necessary, in our opinion, to give its essential characteristics here.

The French government ordered the Marseille Block from Le Corbusier as a prototype. Cost was not a problem. It represents the achievement and the perfection of the vertical city concept developed by Le Corbusier since 1922 in his project for a town of three million inhabitants. The building, situated on a nine acre site on the outskirts of Marseille, has an east-west orientation. It is 450 feet long, 80 feet wide and 185 high.

From a building standpoint, the Marseille Block follows the theoretical principles of Le Corbusier's logic of construction. It has a skeleton of reinforced concrete and rests on powerful *pillars* which leave the ground free. All piping passes through these pillars in order to group longitudinally in a first closed level called "artificial ground." The apartments, all built on two levels, are conceived as individual bottles to be placed in the framework which could be compared to a bottlerack. They are completely standardized, do not touch one another, and are insulated from the framework by the intermediary of lead boxes which assure perfect soundproofing. The northern facade is blank, while the other facades are animated by the *glass walls* and *sunbreak loggias* of the living area.

From the dwelling standpoint, the Radiant City of Marseille expresses Le Corbusier's fundamental preoccupation with satisfying both the collective and individualist aspirations of the human being: with its two levels and its way of insertion into the skeleton, each apartment is like an individual villa, but integrated in a vertical collectivity. This, by virtue of its organizational system, is equivalent, if not superior to, the horizontal collectivities of the classic (residential) quarters of the towns or suburbs.

The Marseille Block contains 337 apartments. They are divided into 23 different types (for single occupants as well as for large families) according to the distribution of their three standard elements, which are: (1) foyer, kitchen, living room; (2) parents' room, bathroom; (3) double room for children, shower and linen room. These apartments (plate 62) are grouped by two's and overlap head to foot along the inside corridors called 'interior streets.' These streets (plate 68), occur every two floors giving access to apartments coupled at the level of the bedrooms (in the case of the apartments called 'upper') or at the level of the living room (in the 'lower' apartments). The living room has a double height of 16 feet, and a glass wall 12 feet in width by 16 feet high. The other rooms, equipped with storage space, are only 8 feet high.

Collective life is favored by a series of common services. On the one hand, of the seven interior streets, two, situated at levels 7 and 8, concentrate commercial stores (food, clothes, pharmacy, hairdresser . . .), the hotel (18 rooms), post office, laundries. On the other hand, at the 18th level, the terrace roof has been provided with a number of facilities for collective use: day nursery, kindergarten, gymnasium for adults, open-air theater and even a 300 meter race track (plates 69, 72, 73).

From an aesthetic point of view, the Radiant City of Marseille illustrates the use of concrete as a noble material. Even its accidents and defects are valued. The powerful and sculptural plastic has a function of expression completed by the use of a violent polychromy. Finally, the Marseille Block is a place of *contrasts* (Cf., the entrance hall, which opposes glass and concrete) and the object of an expert modulation: 15 measures of the Modulor are used to "dimension" these elements.

NOTES TO THE TEXT

1. Le Corbusier was born a year after Mies van der Rohe, and in the same year as Eric Mendelsohn. He is four years younger than Gropius, five years older than Neutra, and eleven years older than Aalto. Frank Lloyd Wright and Auguste Perret were born, respectively, 18 and 13 years before him.

2. La-Chaux-de-Fonds entered the Swiss Confederation only in 1848. Until then, the Comté de Neuchâtel belonged to the Dukes of Nemours et de Longueville. Le Corbusier's forefathers took refuge there during the Albigensian Crusade. They were originally from the Armagnac. For information on Le Corbusier's formative years, consult *L'Art Decoratif d'Aujourd'hui,* the chapter entitled Confession, p. 197.

3. Even now Le Corbusier is never without his sketchbook, an instrument of work and meditation during his trips. Numerous extracts from it have been published, notably in Boesiger's edition of his complete works, and in the special issue of 'Architecture d'Aujourd'hui' published in 1947.

4. Namely, in 1927, on the occasion of the contest for the League of Nations.

5. The analytical summary of 'Esprit Nouveau,' as it appears on the cover:
      Literature, architecture, painting, sculpture, music
      Pure and applied sciences
      Experimental aesthetics, the engineer's aesthetics, town-planning
      Sociological and economical philosophy, moral and political sciences
      Modern life, theater, entertainment, sports, facts.

6. Some names, among others: Aujame, Candilis, Stamo Papadaki, Reidy, Sakakura, R. Salmona, Serralta, J. L. Sert, Soltan Stephenson, Wogenscky, S. Woods, Xenakis.

7. In the U.S.S.R. itself, progressive architecture was defended by the constructivist movement of Tatlin and Malevitch, and boasted some remarkable adherents: A. A. 01, Gunzbourg, J. Kornfeld, Vladimiroff.

8. This pavilion, formed (for reasons of acoustics) entirely of skew surfaces in thin shell concrete (plates 34, 35) will not be mentioned in the following pages: Xenakis's influence prevailed in its conception, which thus does not belong to the aesthetic of Le Corbusier. The latter had himself composed the visual part of the audio-visual show, while musical portion was due to E. Varèse and J. Xenakis.

9. See, for instance, the interpretation of Italian historian Bruno Zevi.

10. Speaking about the Chandigarh building, for example, he says: 'No idea belonging to folk-lore or to the history of art can be taken into consideration in such an enterprise.' Chandigarh is a modern city; the solutions given to its problems will also be modern: reinforced concrete, a new technique, allows us to revolutionize our thinking about the traditional problem of defense against the sun or the torrential rains of the monsoons.

11. The criticism of New York is to be found especially in *When the Cathedrals Were White.* Le Corbusier reproves not only the timidity of the classical skyscrapers he saw in 1935 (before the construction of the Lever building, or the Seagram building), but also their social function: 'The skyscraper here is not an element in city-planning, but a banner in the blue . . . a feather in the cap of a name already listed in the Gotha of money.' To these passionate skyscrapers he op-poses the Cartesian skyscraper.

12. This four-fold classification has become a classic. It is repeated in the Athens Charter, and determines the plan of the book.

13. The first precise project for a rural unit was done in 1934 at the request of a group of inhabitants of the village of Piacé (Sarthe).

14. See text section on Marseille Block.

15. Le Corbusier fights a ruthless war against furniture: cf., 'Don't buy anything but practical furniture, and never decorative furniture. Go and visit the old castles to see the bad taste of the great kings.' *(Towards a New Architecture.)* Modern man, a rational being, free of prejudices and compelled to live in small spaces, will limit himself to minimum equipment: household machines, order-making elements, functional furniture, such as beds, tables, chairs. The majority of Le Corbusier's buildings have also been equipped by him. Starting from 1926, he has perfected his assembly-line furniture with Charlotte Perriand and Pierre Jeanneret.

His criticism of old furniture is also based on a value judgment: in 'decorative' art, the decorative ends up by predominating over the art. 'Hierarchy: first, the Sistine; in other words, works of art in which a passion has really inscribed itself. Afterwards, machines to sit on, machines for classification purposes, lighting machines. . . . To speak truly, decorative art is utensils, beautiful utensils.' ('L'Esprit Nouveau,' No. 23, 1925.)

16. Le Corbusier has introduced to modern architecture a whole vocabulary which today has been universally adopted: corridor streets, pilot plan (a concept born in 1942 in connection with the Project for Algiers, and applied in Bogota in 1950), classified cities, living units, etc.

17. The first project for a museum of continuous growth was dedicated to Ch. Zervos, the director of 'Cahiers d'Art.' The museum is built as the money is made available, around a rec-tangular spiral outlined by standard posts. The interior is structured according to needs by par-titions which are fixed or removable. The museum is without real facades; they exist as a simple dressing which can be removed as the building develops. This idea was taken up again and broadened on the occasion of the Paris Exhibition of 1937.

18. The pillars, which Le Corbusier introduced into modern architecture, were soon, like the sunbreaks, to become, in other hands, the expression of academic stereotype. With pillars and sunbreaks (at times even oriented towards the north), one does 'modern work.'

19. For example, at the Refuge City the Nevade glass bricks exploded, making it impossible for the neutralizing wall to function.

20. The name, carbon-copied from that of the Citroen car, is meant to evoke the idea of assembly-line production.

21. The word, however, horrifies Le Corbusier, who, in the 'Poem of the Right Angle,' writes:

'Functionalism, this horrible word, born under other skies.' 'Machine to live in' is used for the first time in *Towards a New Architecture.*

22. Le Corbusier and the painter Ozenfant, after the 1914 war, created the purist movement, an offshoot of cubism. See: *After Cubism* (1918) and 'L'Esprit Nouveau.'

23. Radiant-towns, architecture of happiness, essential joys, etc. . . .

24. Le Corbusier has also said that the problems of architecture were fundamentally bound up with politics and legislation, and that only a radical reform of the status of real property could, in western societies, put at everyone's disposal the dwellings built according to the predicted standard ideal.

25. The theory of the three most important materials of town planning is discussed again in the Athens Charter, Point 12.

26. Le Corbusier found his ventilation system thanks to his Mediterranean experience. It was in his cabin at Cap Martin, a real 'laboratory of air currents,' that he perfected the device which plays a vital role in Chandigarh. In the Secretariat of this city, the ventilators are in the shape of boxes placed in the undulating glass wall, and closed by sheet-metal shutters 17 inches wide, revolving vertically on their own axes from ceiling to floor, and with an opening of less than $\frac{1}{16}$ of an inch to 17 inches which can be regulated to allow for the most subtle ventilations.

27. The absence of noise is such in the Marseille apartments that some tenants have complained about the silence.

28. The collectivity-individuality twosome is one of Le Corbusier's great themes: it guides all his architecture and town planning. There is a perpetual counterpoint between these two aspects. The example of monastic life furnished him with the archetype of this double polarity, which struck him for the first time in 1907 at the Charter House of Ema in Tuscany.

29. In cities, the high price of land compels one to live in a small space.

30. The cabin (1952) consists of one room, about 12 feet on a side and seven and one half feet high. It provides for the functions of sleep and rest (two beds and chairs), work (table and bookshelves), hygiene (wash basin and toilet) and storage (the suitcases and cumbersome objects are stored in a double ceiling). In 1923, Le Corbusier had already built for his parents a small, ideal house of 580 square feet.

31. It is amusing to note Le Corbusier's annoyance with clients who do not use their houses according to his intent. So, for instance, the occupants of the Jaoul houses made the 'mistake' of installing old furniture which they were fond of.

The belief in the identity of reaction of all men is expressed in striking formulas like this: 'Human needs are very few; they are identical in all people, since all people have been cast in the same mould since the earliest times we know of. . . . These needs can be reduced to a number of types, which means that we all have the same needs.' ('L'Esprit Nouveau,' No. 23, 1925.)

32. 'L'Esprit Nouveau,' No. 23.

33. *Toward a New Architecture,* Chapter: The Illusion of Plans.

34. 'One can count only on targets accessible to the eye; (otherwise one arrives at) the illusion of plans' *(Towards a New Architecture).*

35. This relativity of spatial perception leads him to the development of the *inexpressible space* theory.

36. The first book on the Modulor was published in 1948. It was immediately translated into four languages and used by architects the world over. If Le Corbusier calculates all his modules with this instrument, it seems that it must be the formalization of an instinct which from the

beginning harmonized in an infallible way the dimensions of the Swiss Pavilion or of the La Roche house with the human scale.

37. In Marseille Le Corbusier uses 15 units of the Modulor.

38. See especially those of the High Court of Chandigarh, of the Sarabhai house, or of the Brazilian Pavilion. They received the name of *optimum paving.*

39. Cf., 'A house which is this human limit encircling us, and separating us from the antagonistic natural phenomenon' *(Towards a New Architecture,* Introduction to the second edition) or 'The horizons must be reconquered' *(The Home of Man)* or 'The plan conquers the landscape' *(Crusade).* In *A Little House,* Le Corbusier tells how he structures the landscape by building a wall around the little house he constructed for his parents. 'One must limit the landscape, give it dimensions by a radical decision. . . .'

40. One can see, for example, on the Marseille terrace or under the pillars of the House of Brazil (in the rainwater pipes), the refined masonry work meant to contrast with the roughness of the brute concrete which dominates in the two buildings.

41. Seen especially in Marseille and in the Ministries of Chandigarh.

42. We are thinking of the aesthetic of a Dubuffet, for example.

43. These sculptures are executed after the drawings of Savina, cabinet-maker from Brittany.

44. The principal door of Ronchamp is of enameled steel, and has compositions by Le Corbusier on both sides.

45. This is rigorously purist, and until 1928 analyzes simple objects. Then Le Corbusier starts to become interested in what he calls *objects which evoke a poetic reaction* (fragments of roots, bones, shells). At the same time, the human figure is introduced in his work and he does realist portraits and paints big bathing women who remind one a little of Picasso's neo-classic period. Afterwards, one witnesses a liberation in forms, which become almost abstract and inter-penetrate even more. This evolution is the more significant since, according to Le Corbusier himself, the painter's search for forms has never ceased to support the work of the architect.

46. This will be the case even with poured concrete furniture which has lately acquired a singular nobility. See especially the tables of the Brazilian Pavilion.

47. The function of rigorous and brutal exterior delineation of forms attributed to light is a Mediterranean heritage. Le Corbusier's architecture is an architecture of the Mediterranean, a sea for which he has always suffered what he calls 'an invincible attraction' *(Crusade).*

48. The openings pierced in the Ronchamp walls of different widths. They contribute to the general plastic effect, are provided with glass, colored or not, on which, in a spirit opposed to that of stained-glass which belongs to another time, Le Corbusier has painted symbols.

49. The examples of interior polychromy are quite numerous in Le Corbusier's work. Cf., Marseille, Nantes, Brazilian Pavilion, the Jaoul villa, workshops of the St. Dié factory.

50. This aesthetic appears independently of the use of concrete when Le Corbusier is compelled by circumstances to use traditional materials (wood or stone), as in the Errazuris house in Chile (1930), or in the Mathes house.

51. In Nantes, the pillars were calculated as closely as possible in order to economize in comparison with Marseille. They are much less massive, and also less expressive.

52. 'A Gothic cathedral interests us as an ingenious solution to a difficult problem, the data of which were badly set because they did not proceed from the great primary forms. The cathedral is no plastic work; it is a drama: the struggle against gravity, a sensation of sentimental order.' *(Towards a New Architecture.)*

53. See especially the houses of Jaoul or Sarabhai.

54. The *musical or undulated* glass walls are glass surfaces with fine ribs of reinforced concrete. Their name comes from the fact that the ribs are arranged in a complex relationship, calculated according to the Modulor and comparable to musical relations.

55. The knob on the main door, as well as the benches of Ronchamp, the poured con-crete shower rooms of the Brazilian Pavilion, as well as the solution of continuity between stairs and the adjacent wall at the Jaoul house and at the Brazilian Pavilion, among others, have all been the objects of detailed elaboration.

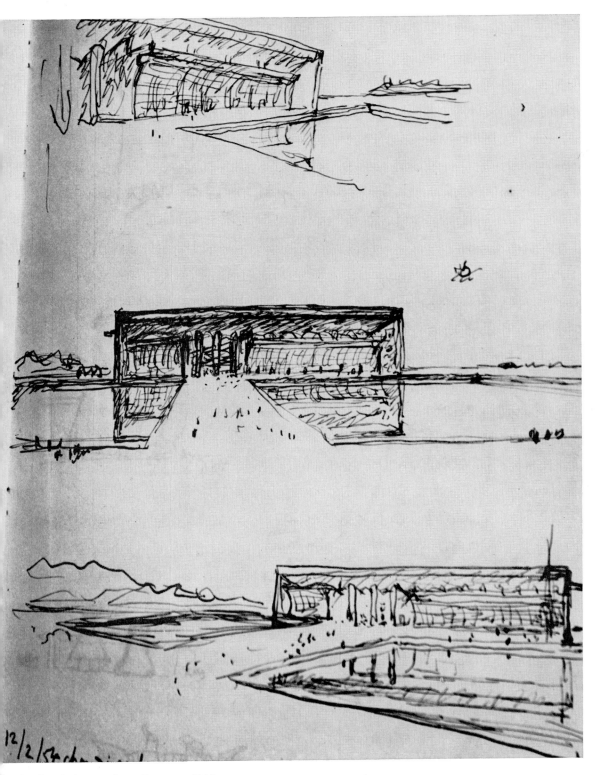

1. Sketches during a Trip to Greece, c. 1910.

2. Villa, Vaucresson, 1922.

3. La Roche House, Paris, 1923.

4. Cook House, Paris, 1926. Exterior detail.

5. Villa Garches, 1927. Front view.

6. Savoye Villa, Poissy, 1929–1931.

7. Savoye Villa.

8. Savoye Villa.

9. Palace of the Soviets, 1931. Model of project.

10. Workers' Housing, Pessac, 1925.

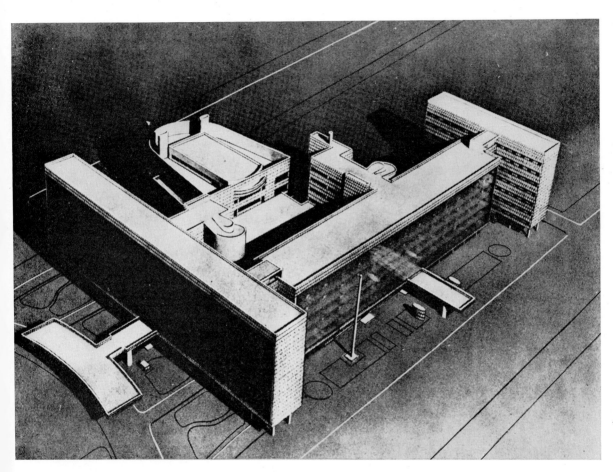

11. Centrosoyus, Moscow, 1928–35.

12. Swiss Pavilion, University City, Paris, 1930–32.

13. Swiss Pavilion (opposite page).

14. Swiss Pavilion.

15. Swiss Pavilion.

16. Brazilian Pavilion, University City, Paris, 1956–59.

17. Ministry of National Education, Rio de Janiero,
1936–1945.

18. Voisin Plan for Paris, 1922. Model.

19. Voisin Plan for Paris, 1925. Model.

20. Traffic Plan for Algiers, 1931, 1934, 1938.

21. Building and Gardens, Algiers, 1930.

22. Plan for Algiers, 1930. Model.

23. St. Dié, 1945. Town plan.

24. Skyscraper for Algiers, 1938–1942. Model of project.

25. Jaoul House, Neuilly, 1952--56. Living room of Villa A.

26. Jaoul House, View of the two levels.

27. Jaoul House. Living room of Villa B.

28 Villa Sarabhai, Ahmedabad, India, 1955-56

29. Villa Sarabhai. Interior.

30. Duval Works, St. Dié, 1946–1951. Exterior.

31. Duval Works. Workshops.

32. Tokyo Museum, Japan, 1956. Model.

33. Museum of the "Square Spiral," 1939. Model of project.

34. Philips Pavilion, Brussels International Fair, 1958. Exterior detail.

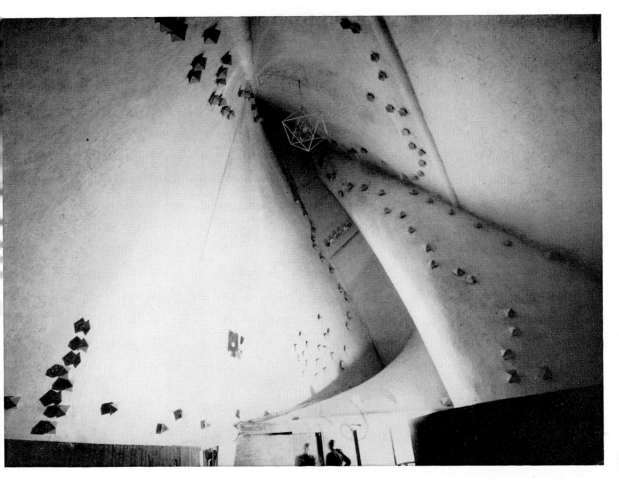

35. Philips Pavilion. Interior detail.

36. Chapel, Ronchamp, 1950–55.

37. Chapel, Ronchamp. View from South.

38. Chapel, Ronchamp. View from South-East.

9. Chapel, Ronchamp. Exterior, outdoor pulpit.

40. Chapel, Ronchamp. View from North-East.

41. Chapel, Ronchamp. Interior.

42. Chapel, Ronchamp. Interior toward rear.

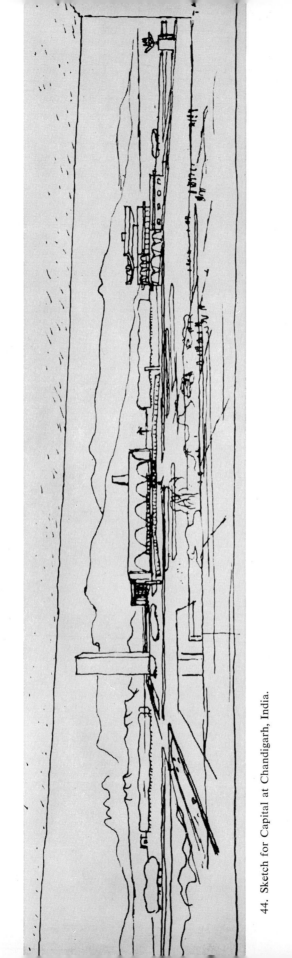

44. Sketch for Capital at Chandigarh, India.

45. High Court Building, Chandigarh, India. Sketch, 12/2/54, showing pool basins.

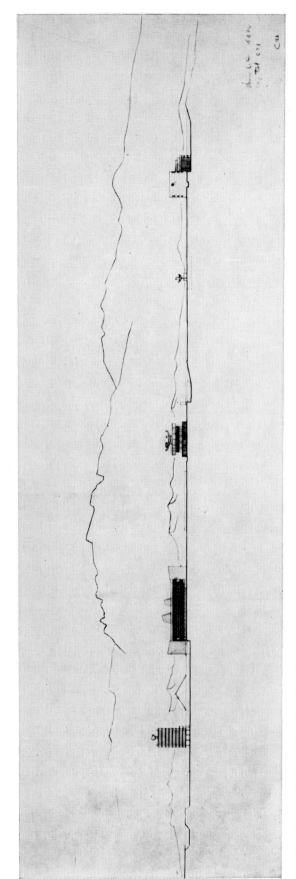

46. Drawing for the Capital at Chandigarh.

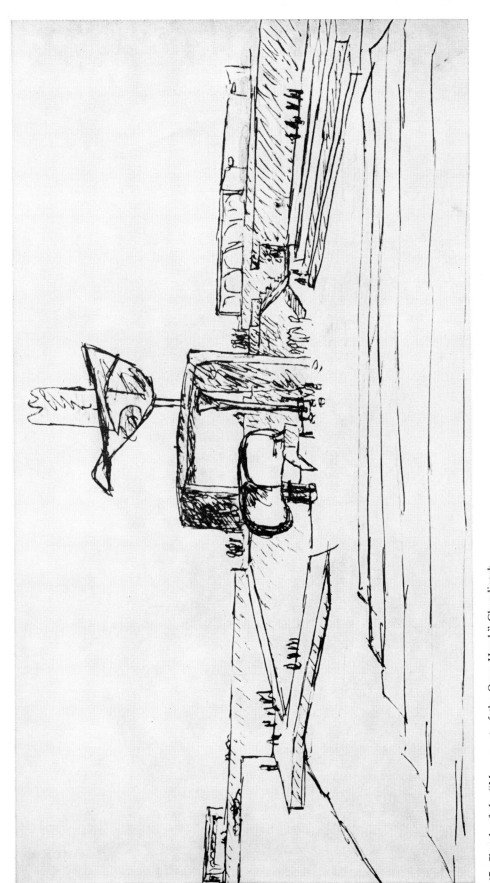

47. Sketch of the "Monument of the Open Hand," Chandigarh.

Le Corbusier: Secretariat Building, Chandigarh, India, 1951-56

49. High Court Building, Chandigarh.

50. High Court Building, Chandigarh. Exterior showing sunbreaks.

51. High Court Building, Chandigarh. Exterior detail.

53. High Court Building, Chandigarh. Inclined ramps.

52. High Court Building, Chandigarh. Detail of ramps (opposite page).

54. Secretariat, Chandigarh, India, 1951–56. Exterior.

55. Secretariat, Chandigarh. Exterior detail.

56. Secretariat, Chandigarh. Detail.

57. Secretariat, Chandigarh. Interior detail.

58. Marseille Block, 1947–1952.

59. Marseille Block. Exterior.

60. Marseille Block. View from North-West showing firestair.

61. Marseille Block. Detail from southeast.

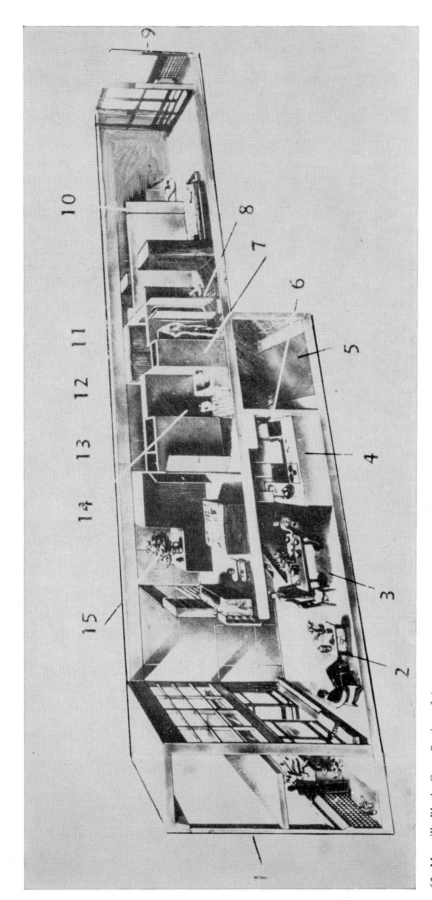

62. Marseille Block. Cross-Section of Apartment.

63. Marseille Block. Detail of kitchen.

64. Marseille Block. View of living room toward kitchen.

65. Marseille Block. Apartment interior.

66. Marseille Block. View of interior toward terrace.

67. Marseille Block. Sun-break over terrace.

68. Marseille Block. Interior street.

69. Marseille Block. Roof nursery.

70. Marseille Block. Detail of columns.

71. Marseille Block. View of columns.

72. Marseille Block. Roof swimming pool.

73. Marseille Block. Roof (theatre, ventilation chimney, gymnasium).

74. Marseille Block. Roof detail.

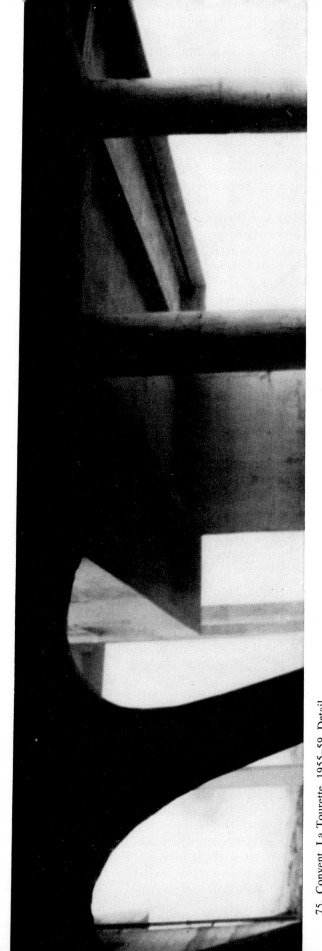

75. Convent, La Tourette, 1955–59. Detail.

76. Convent, La Tourette. Detail showing columns.

77. Convent, La Tourette. Exterior detail.

78. Convent La Tourette. Exterior detail of upper facade.

79. Le Corbusier retouching the painting *Still-Life with Various Objects,* 1923. Museum of Modern Art, Paris.

80. *Still-Life with Various Objects.*

81. *Still-Life with Various Objects*. Detail of left-center section.

82. *Still-Life with Various Objects.* Detail of lower section to the right center.

83. Brazilian Pavilion, University City, Paris, 1956–59. Director's apartment, facade detail showing exterior ventilators.

84. Convent, La Tourette. Facade detail showing exterior ventilators.

85. Nantes Block, Nantes-Rezé 1952–55. Exterior detail of facade reliefs.

86. Marseille Block, 1947–1952. Le Corbusier and Modulor relief.

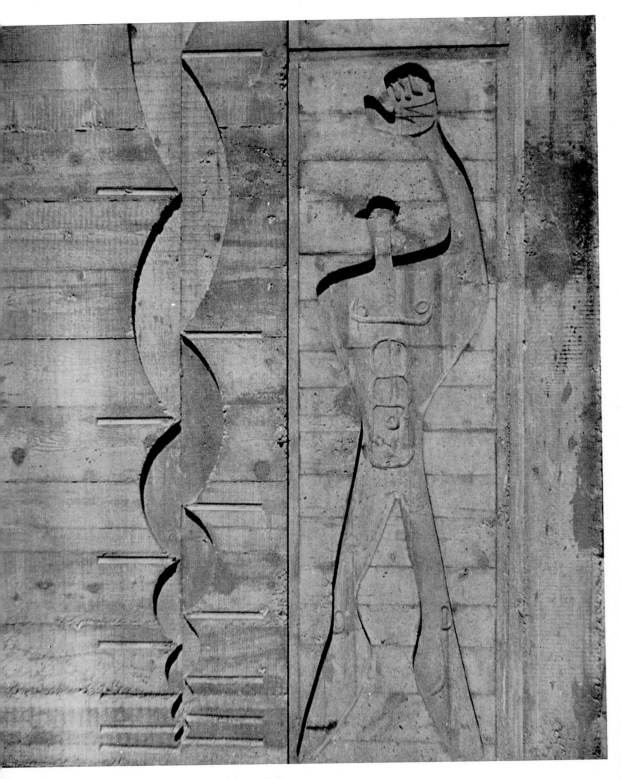

87. Marseille Block, 1947–1952. Modulor relief.

SELECTED BIBLIOGRAPHY

THE BASIC work indispensable for a profound knowledge of Le Corbusier is: LE CORBUSIER, Complete Works, published by Boesiger in the Girsberger Editions (Zurich).

Boesiger has undertaken the complete photographic publication of Le Corbusier's architectural work and plans. The collection is completed by important Le Corbusier texts and by numerous reproductions of his drawings, paintings, tapestries and sculpture. Six volumes have already appeared, covering the periods from 1910–1929, 1929–1934, 1934–1938, 1938–46, 1952–1957.

LE CORBUSIER'S WORKS

Towards a New Architecture, Editions Crès, Paris, 1923, republished by Vincent Fréal, Paris, 1959.
Modern Painting (in collaboration with Ozenfant and under the name Jeanneret), Editions Crès, Paris, 1925, republished by Vincent Fréal, Paris, 1959.
The Decorative Art of Today, Editions Crès, Paris, 1925, republished by Vincent Fréal, Paris, 1959.
Town Planning, Editions Crès, Paris, 1925.
Almanac of Modern Architecture, Editions Crès, Paris, 1927.
A House, A Palace, Editions Crès, Paris, 1928.
Clarifications, Editions Crès, Paris, 1930.
Crusade, Editions Crès, Paris, 1932.
The Radiant City, Architecture d'Aujourd'hui, Paris, 1935.
Air Craft, Ed. The Studio, London, 1935.
When the Cathedrals Were White, Ed. Plon, Paris, 1937.
Guns, Ammunition? Thank you! Dwellings... Please, Ed. de l'Architecture d'Aujourd'hui, Paris, 1938.
The Lyricism of New Times and Town Planning, Ed. du Point, Colmar, 1939.
The Destiny of Paris, Editions Sorlot, Paris, 1941.
On the Four Roads, Editions Gallimard, Paris, 1941.
The Home of Man (in collaboration with F. de Pierrefeu), Ed. Plon, Paris, 1942.
Exchange of Views with Students of the Schools of Architecture, Ed. Denoel, Paris, 1943, reissued by Editions de Minuit, Paris, 1957.
The Athens Charter, Ed. Plon, Paris, 1943, republished by Editions de Minuit, 1957.
The Three Human Establishments, Ed. Denoel, Paris, 1944. Reissued by Editions de Minuit, Paris, 1959.
Concerning Town Planning, Ed. Bourrelier, Paris, 1946.
U. N. Headquarters, Reinhold, New York, 1947.
New World of Space, Reynal & Hitchcock, New York, 1948.

The Marseille Block, Le Point, Souilhac, 1950.
The Modulor 1948, Architecture d'Aujourd'hui, Paris, 1950.
The Poem of the Right Angle, Verve, Paris, 1953.
The Modulor 2, Architecture d'Aujourd'hui, Paris, 1954.
A Little House, Girsberger, Zurich, 1954.
The Le Corbusier Plans for Paris, Editions de Minuit, Paris, 1956.
Ronchamp, Girsberger, Zurich, 1957.
The Electronic Poem, Editions de Minuit, Paris, 1958.

WORKS ON LE CORBUSIER

Architecture d'Aujourd'hui, special Le Corbusier and Pierre Jeanneret issue, 1933.
Architecture d'Aujourd'hui, special issue on Le Corbusier's 60th birthday, April, 1948.
Alazard, Jean, *Le Corbusier,* Electra, Florence, 1951.
Gauthier, Maximilien, *Le Corbusier, or the Architect in the Service of Man,* Denoel, Paris, 1944.
Giedion, Siegfried, *Le Corbusier and Contemporary Architecture,* Cahiers d'Art, Paris, 1930.
Henze, Anton, *Le Corbusier,* Colloquium, Berlin, 1957.
Jardot, Maurice, *Le Corbusier* (Drawings), Editions des Deux Mondes, Paris, 1955.
Papadaki, Stamo, in collaboration with J. Hudnut, F. Léger, J. L. Sert, S. Giedion, J. J. Soby, *Le Corbusier, Architect, Painter, Writer,* MacMillan, New York, 1941.
Persico, Edoardo, "Introduction to Le Corbusier" in *Casabella* No. 85, 1933.

One can also consult the passages concerning Le Corbusier in the following works:

Hitchcock, H.-R., *Architecture of the Nineteenth & Twentieth Centuries,* Penguin Books, London, 1959.
Giedion, S., *Space, Time and Architecture,* Harvard University Press, Cambridge, USA, 1941.
————, *A Decade of Contemporary Architecture,* Zurich, 1954.
Zevi, Bruno, *Storia dell'architettura Moderna* (The History of Modern Architecture), Einaudi, Milan, 1950.

LIFE AND WORKS OF LE CORBUSIER

1886
1887   Birth of Charles-Edouard Jeanneret at La Chaux-de-Fonds (Switzerland)
1889
1891
1896
1898
1900   Leaves Elementary School to serve his apprenticeship as an engraver-chiseler at the
        Art School at La Chaux-de-Fonds
1902
1904–5 BUILDS HIS FIRST HOUSE IN HIS NATIVE VILLAGE
1905
1906   Beginning of the knapsack-trips period
1907
1908   Arrival in Paris. Work in Auguste Perret's studio
1910–11 Trip to Germany. Behrens's studio
1913
1914–15 (Domino prefabricated houses with independent skeleton)
1919
1920   Foundation of the magazine L'Esprit Nouveau with Ozenfant and Paul Dermée
1922   With his cousin Pierre Jeanneret he opens the atelier at 35 *rue de Sèvres*. The Citrohan
        house (No. 2) destined to be mass produced.
1923   *Towards a New Architecture*
1924
1925   ESPRIT NOUVEAU PAVILION
        (First Voisin Plan for Paris)
1925–26 Pessac development, Gironde

* Books are *italics,* buildings are in CAPITAL LETTERS, projects are in (parentheses).

SUMMARY *

MAIN EVENTS IN CONTEMPORARY ARCHITECTURE

Birth of Mies van der Rohe	1886
Paris Universal Exhibition. EIFFEL TOWER	1889
BEGINNING OF THE SAGRADA FAMILIA BY GAUDÍ IN BARCELONA	1891
HORTA, THE PEOPLE'S HOUSE IN BRUSSELS	1896
Alvar Aalto's birth	1898
BEGINNING OF GAUDÍ'S GÜELL PARK IN BARCELONA	1900
PERRET BUILDS THE FIRST HOUSE WITH A CONCRETE SKELETON, RUE FRANKLIN, PARIS	1902
PONTHIEU GARAGE BY PERRET	1905
F. L. WRIGHT, ROBERTS HOUSE, RIVER FOREST, ILLINOIS	1907
Birth of Eero Saarinen	1910
FAGUS FACTORY BY GROPIUS AT ALFELD-AU-DER-LEINE, GERMANY	1913
FREYSSINET'S PLANE HANGARS AT ORLY, FRANCE	1914
Weimar Bauhaus founded by Gropius	1919
RIETVELD, UTRECHT VILLA, NETHERLANDS	1924
International Exhibition of Decorative Arts, in Paris	1925
Second Bauhaus established by Gropius at Dessau, Germany	1925

1927	(Project for the League of Nations Palace at Geneva)
1928	Takes part in the foundation and establishes the discussion project for the first CIAM Congress at La Sarraz (Switzerland)
1929	BEGINNING OF THE CENTROSOYUS IN MOSCOW, TO BE FINISHED IN 1935
1930	Becomes a French citizen
1930–31	SAVOYE HOUSE AT POISSY
1931	(Museum of unlimited growth [square spiral])
	(Palace of the Soviets, Moscow)
1932	SWISS PAVILION AT THE PARIS CITÉ UNIVERSITAIRE
1933	Takes part in the 4th Congress of the CIAM in Athens, at which the Athens Charter is drawn up
	(Town planning map for the city of Anvers)
	(Apartment house project at Algiers with the first sunbreak)
1934	
1935	First trip to the U.S., on which he based *When the Cathedrals Were White* (published in 1937)
1936	COLLABORATES IN THE PLANS FOR THE MINISTRY OF NATIONAL EDUCATION IN RIO DE JANEIRO
1937	
1938	(Master Plan for Buenos Aires)
1942	Writing and publication of the Athens Charter
1943	
1945	(Town planning project for Saint Dié)
1946	
1947–51	THE MARSEILLE BLOCK
1948	
1950	(Town planning project for Bogotá)
	Modulor T 1
1951	He is entrusted with the construction and town planning of Chaṇdigarh, the new capital of Punjab, India
1952	CHANDIGARH PALACE OF JUSTICE (FINISHED IN 1956)
1953	Le Corbusier Exhibition at the Museum of Modern Art, Paris
1955	FINISHES THE NOTRE-DAME DU HAUT CHURCH AT RONCHAMPS, FRANCE
1956	SHODAN VILLA AT AHMEDABAD, INDIA
1958	PHILIPS PAVILION AT BRUSSELS INTERNATIONAL FAIR
1959	INAUGURATION OF THE BRAZILIAN PAVILION AT THE PARIS CITÉ UNIVERSITAIRE

FIRST PREFABRICATED DYMAXION HOUSE BY BUCKMINSTER FULLER	1927
MIES VAN DER ROHE, PAVILION AT THE INTERNATIONAL EXHIBITION IN BARCELONA	1928
NEUTRA, LOVELL HOUSE IN LOS ANGELES	1929
HOOD, DAILY NEWS SKYSCRAPER IN NEW YORK	1930
ROCKEFELLER CENTER, NEW YORK	1931
AALTO, PAIMIO SANATORIUM, FINLAND	1932
AALTO, VIIPURI LIBRARY, FINLAND	1934
TORROJA, MADRID STADIUM	1935
F. L. WRIGHT, "FALLING WATER," KAUFMANN HOUSE AT BEAR RUN, PENNSYLVANIA	1936
F. L. WRIGHT, JOHNSON WAX FACTORY AT RACINE, WISCONSIN	1937
NERVI, MILITARY HANGARS AT ORBETELLO, ITALY	1938
J. PROUVE, METAL CURTAIN-WALL AT THE COVERED MARKET, CLICHY, FRANCE	1938
MIES VAN DER ROHE, BUILDING FOR MINERALOGICAL AND METALLURGICAL RESEARCH AT THE ILLINOIS INSTITUTE OF TECHNOLOGY, CHICAGO, ILLINOIS	1942
COMPLETION OF THE MINISTRY OF NATIONAL EDUCATION IN RIO DE JANEIRO, BRAZIL BY NIEMEYER, COSTA, REIDY, MOREIRA AND LEAO	1943
F. L. WRIGHT, PROJECT FOR THE GUGGENHEIM MUSEUM, NEW YORK, FINISHED IN 1959	1946
NEUTRA, TREMAINE HOUSE, CALIFORNIA	1948
AALTO, SÄYNÄTSALO TOWN HALL, FINLAND	1950
EERO SAARINEN BEGINS THE GENERAL MOTORS TECHNICAL INSTITUTE, DETROIT, WHICH WILL BE FINISHED IN 1955	1951
MIES VAN DER ROHE, LAKE SHORE DRIVE APARTMENTS IN CHICAGO	1951
BUNSCHAFT, LEVER HOUSE, NEW YORK	1952
CANDELA, NUESTRA SEÑORA DE LOS MILAGROS CHURCH IN MEXICO CITY (FINISHED IN 1955)	1953
Brussels International Fair	1958

All of the photographs in this book are by Lucien Hervé, Paris.

INDEX

The numerals in *italics* refer to the illustrations.

Aalto, 16

After Cubism (Le Corbusier), 29

Ahmedabad, India, Shodan villa, 13; Villa Sarabhai, 13, *28–29*

Air conditioning, 17

Algiers, 12, 15, *20–24*

Allendy, R., 11

Anvers, Belgium, 12

Apartment, Marseille block, *62–65*

Athens Charter, 12

Barcelona, Spain, 12, 19

Bauhaus, 11

Beams, concrete, 24

Behrens, 10

Berlin, Interbau, 12

Brazil, Ministry of National Education, 12, 17, *17*

Brazilian Pavilion, University City, Paris, 12, 19, 23, 31, *16, 83*

Bricks, glass, 28

Briey-la-Forêt, 13

Brussels International Fair, Philips Pavilion, 13, *34–35*

Brutality, 24

Buildings and Gardens, Algiers, *21*

Buildings, concrete, Chandigarh, 13–14 large, plans for, 12

"Cahiers d'Art," 28

Candela, 23

Capitol, Chandigarh, 13, *44, 46*

Cap Martin, cabin, 10, 20

Cell, dwelling, 16. *See also* Dwelling unit

Centrosoyus, Moscow, 12, 17, *11*

Chandigarh, India, Capitol, 13, *44, 46;* High Court building, 13, 22, 23, *48–53;* sunbreak, 17; Secretariat, 17, 19, 29, *54–57*

Chapel, Ronchamp, 13, 20, 23, 30, *36–43*

Charreau, Pierre, 12

Charter House, Ema Tuscany, 29

C.I.A.M., 12

Citrohan house, 17, 18

Color, use of, 23

Columns, *70–71, 76*

Comté de Neuchâtel, 27

Concrete, 23; reinforced, 10, 16; buildings, 13–14; beams, 24; poured, 30

Constructivist movement, 27

Convent, La Tourette, 13, 19, *75–78, 84*

Cook house, Paris, 12, 17, 22, *4*

Critical analysis, Le Corbusier's, 14–16

Crusade (Le Corbusier), 11, 30

Cubism, 18

Dautry, Raoul, 13

De Mandrot villa, 21

Dermée, Charles, 11

Domino houses, 11, 18

Drawing for the capitol at Chandigarh, India, *46*

Drew, Jane, 13

Dubuffet, 30
Duval works, St. Dié, 13, 18, *23, 30–31;* facade, 21; ceiling, 24
Dwelling unit, 15–16, 20

Ecole des Beaux-Arts, 10
Ema, Tuscany, Charter House, 29
Equipment, functional, 16
Errazuris house, Chile, 21, 30
"Esprit Nouveau," 11, 29

Firestair, Marseille block, *60*
Fourier, 19
Free plan, 16
Frescoes, 22
Fry, Maxwell, 13
Functionalism, 14
Functions, 15; individual and collective, 16
Furniture, 16, 28; poured concrete, 30

Garches house, 22
Garden, suspended, 18
Gardens, Algiers, *21*
Garden towns, 15
Gaudí, 18
Glass, wall, 16, 31; inserted in concrete, 24; bricks, 28
Gothic cathedral, 30
Greece, 10, 20, *1*
Gropius, 11, 16

Hertz, H., 11
High Court building, Chandigarh, India, 13, 23, *45, 48–54*
Home of Man (Le Corbusier), 30
Housing, prefabricated, 11, 18
Housing unit, vertical, 16

Industrial design, 11
Interior lighting, 23
Interior streets, 18, 26, *68*
International Congresses of Modern Architecture, 12

Jaoul house, Neuilly, 13, 17, 19, 23, 31, *27–27*
Jeanneret, Albert, 11

Jeanneret, Charles Edouard. *See* Le Corbusier
Jeanneret, Pierre, 11, 13, 28
Jeanneret family, 9–10

La-Chaux-de-Fonds, 9; Art School, 10, 11
Laffaille, 23
La Roche house, Paris, 12, 16, *3*
La Rochelle. *See* Rochelle
La Tourette convent, 13, 19, *75–78, 84*
League of Nations Palace, Geneva, 12
Le Corbusier (Charles Edouard Jeanneret), 9; Paris studio, 11; "The Plan for a Contemporary City of Three Million Inhabitants," 16; *After Cubism,* 29; "Poem of the Right Angle," 29; *Crusade,* 11, 30; *The Home of Man,* 30; *A Little House,* 30; *When the Cathedrals Were White,* 28; retouching *Still-Life with Various Objects, 79;* and Modulor relief, *86*
Léger, Fernand, 18
L'Eplatenier, 10
Light, use of, 23
Linear industrial city, 15
Lipschitz, 22
Little House (Le Corbusier), 30
Lurçat, Jean, 11

Malevitch, 27
Mallet-Stevens, 12
Mansions, private, 13
Marseille block, 13, 16, 17, 20, 23, 25–26, *58–74, 86–87;* Modulor, 30
Masonry, stone, 21; coated, 24
Masses, organization of, 22
Materials, deterioration of, 18; natural, 21
Mathes house, 19, 21, 30
Meaux, France, 13
Mechanism, 14–18
Mediterranean, 30
Mies van der Rohe, 18
Milhaud, Darius, 11
Ministry of National Education, Rio de Janeiro, 12, 17, *17*
Modulor, 20, 26, 30; relief, *86–87*
Moscow, Centrosoyus, 12, 17, *11*

Museum, Tokyo, 13, *32*
Museum of the "Square Spiral," *33*
Nantes block, Nantes-Rezé, 13, *85*
Nature, vegetation, 21
Nervi, 23
Neuilly, Jaoul house, 13, 17, 19, 31, *25–27*
New York city, 15, 28

Ozenfant, Amédée, 11, 29; house, Paris, 12

Palace of the Soviets, *9*
Paris, La Roche house, 3, 12, 16; Cook house, 12, 17, 22, *4;* first building with concrete framework, 10; Ozenfant house, 12; University City, 12, *12–16, 83;* Salvation Army Refuge City, 12, 17, 28; Voisin plan, 12, *18–19;* plan for, 15
Perret, Auguste, 10
Perriand, Charlotte, 28
Pessac, Workers' housing, 12, *10*
Petit, Claudius, 13
Philips Pavilion, Brussels International Fair, 13, *34–35*
Picasso, 30
Piles, supporting, 16, 17
Pillar foundation (pilotis), 16
Plan for Algiers, *22*
"Plan for a Contemporary City of Three Million Inhabitants," (Le Corbusier), 16
"Poem of the Right Angle" (Le Corbusier), 29
Poissy, France, Villa Savoye, 17, *6–8*
Pool basins, Chandigarh, India, *45*
Prefabricated houses, 11, 18
Punjab, capital, 13. *See also* Chandigarh
Purist movement, 29

Radio-concentric city, 15
Ramps, Chandigarh, *52–53*
Rationalism, 14–18
Raynal, Maurice, 11
Refuge City of the Salvation Army, Paris, 12, 17; glass bricks, 28
Reliefs, *85–87*
Rietveld, 12
Rio de Janeiro, Brazil, Ministry of National Education, 12, 17, *17*

Rochelle-Pallice, France, 13, 15
Ronchamp chapel, 13, 20, 23, 36–43; principal door, 30
Roof, umbrella, 13, 22; terrace, 16, 17–18; ascending curve, 20; double curve, 22; nursery, *69;* swimming pool, *72*

Saint Dié, Duval works, 13, 17, 21, 23, 24, *30–31*
Salvation Army, Refuge City, 12, 17, 28
Sarabhai villa, Ahmedabad, India, 13, *28–29*
Sarraz Castle, Switzerland, 12
Savoye villa, Poissy, 17, *6–8*
Sculpture, 22
Secretariat, Chandigarh, 13, 19, *54–57;* ventilators, 29
Shodan villa, Ahmedabad, 13
Skeleton, independent, 16
Sketches during a trip to Greece, *1*
Skyscrapers, 13, 28; for Algiers, *24*
Soundproofing, 19, 25
Soviets, Palace of, *9*
Space, illusions created by, 20
"Square Spiral," Museum of the, *33*
Staircase, exterior, 23
Steel, and reinforced concrete, 16
Still-Life with Various Objects, 80–82
Stockholm, 12
Stone, masonry, 21; and contrasting materials, 24
Streets, interior, 18, 26, *68*
Sunbreaks, 13, 16, *50, 67*
Swimming pool, roof, *72*
Swiss Pavilion, University City, Paris, 12, 17, 20, *12–15*

Tapestry, 22
Tatlin, 27
Tokyo Museum, 13, *32*
Towards a New Architecture (Le Corbusier), 11, 30
Town-planning, 11, 12, 25–26; unit of, 20
Towns, functions and traffic, 16
Traffic, system, 15–16; plan for Algiers, *20*

Umbrella roofs, 13, 22

UNESCO Secretariat, Paris (Nervi), 23
Unit of agricultural exploitation, 15
Universal man, 19
University City, Paris, 12, 17, 20, *12–16, 83*

Vaucresson, villa, 12, 22, *2*
Ventilation, 18
Ventilators, *83–84*
Vertical city, 19, 25
Villa Garches, *5*
Villa Sarabhai, Ahmedabad, 13, *28–29*

Villa, Vaucresson, 12, 22, *2*
Voisin plan, Paris, 12, *18–19*

Wanderjahre, 10
When the Cathedrals Were White (Le Corbusier), 28
Window, continuous bands, 17
Workers' housing, Pessac, 12, *10*

Zervos, Ch., 28